"In a world where su—
leads families throu—
Christ. With warmth
and Suffering invites weary hearts to find a gospel hope—one that is
honest about sorrow yet unwavering in Christ's steadfast love. For
families facing sorrow, these pages offer comfort, gospel hope, and
the faithful love of Christ."
    Darby Strickland, Faculty, Christian Counseling &
    Educational Foundation; author, *Something Sad Happened*

"Tackling tough topics such as pain and suffering and responding
to common questions for both teens and adults require remarkable
skill. Beth Broom makes a difficult area of theology understandable
and practical. Written with both theological depth and a counselor's
heart and eyes, this book will serve a variety of people and audiences."
    Jonathan Holmes, Executive Director, Fieldstone Counseling

"*10 Questions About Pain and Suffering* is a remarkably honest and
helpful guide for kids, teenagers, families—anyone, really. Beth
Broom walks us through difficult questions, addressing them head-
on with great care and humility. Each question is given the space
for earnest and multifaceted reflection, with answers and discus-
sion flowing out in successive layers of biblical truth and wisdom."
    Scott James, MD, author, *The Sower; The Expected One;*
    When Your Child Is Ill; and *Deep Breath, Little Whisper*

"Speaking directly to kids, teens, and families, this devotional-style
book puts God's love and comfort on full display amid our hardest
moments. Beth Broom doesn't just help readers understand suffering; she shows us how to find hope and healing in the middle of
it. Whether your family is going through a tough time or you just
want to understand why bad things happen, this book will not only
inspire meaningful conversations in your home but will help you
feel God's closeness and care."
    Eliza Huie, author, *Raising Emotionally Healthy Kids;*
    Trauma Aware; and *Count Yourself Calm*

"We live in a broken world. Children and teens are not immune from shards of this brokenness impacting their lives. Beth Broom provides brief, accessible devotions to help young people be less disoriented by the suffering they face. Parents will appreciate the conversations these 10 Questions devotional prompts provide. If you want to protect the faith of your children, don't leave them ignorant about how to face suffering."

Brad Hambrick, Pastor of Counseling, The Summit Church, Durham, North Carolina; author, *Angry with God: An Honest Journey Through Suffering and Betrayal*

"Beth Broom offers clear, biblical comfort for kids who are going through pain and suffering. In this devotional, she walks through the main questions people ask as they experience times of pressure and difficulty, pointing readers continually to God as the ultimate source of comfort and rest. This will be a trusted resource I constantly reuse as a counselor and parent!"

Joseph Hussung, Director of Ministry Partnerships and Recruitment, Fieldstone Counseling; author, *Learning to Listen: Essential Skills for Every Counselor*

"Genesis 3 is the common denominator of life in this fallen world. Everyone, including kids, experiences suffering, pain, and sadness. But there is hope. I'm thankful for Beth Broom's work in this honest, theologically rich, enjoyable, and accessible book. *10 Questions About Pain and Suffering* shows the compounding hope of the gospel that continues to be good news for sinners and sufferers."

J. A. Medders, Director of Theology and Content, Send Network; author, *Humble Calvinism*

"Saturated with Scripture and written in a wonderfully accessible way, Beth Broom's *10 Questions About Pain and Suffering* is loaded with helpful guidance for the whole family on a particularly tough topic. Built on the timeless truths of God's word, this book offers clarity and practical help to see God's heart in the midst of pain and suffering."

    Andrew Dealy, Executive Director, Austin Stone Counseling Center; Founder and CEO, Ever Rise Care & Consulting

10 Questions About Pain and Suffering

10 Questions

Edited by Champ Thornton

10 Questions About Pain and Suffering, Beth M. Broom

10 Questions About Salvation, Champ Thornton

10 QUESTIONS ABOUT PAIN AND SUFFERING

30 Devotions for Kids, Teens, and Families

Beth M. Broom

WHEATON, ILLINOIS

10 Questions About Pain and Suffering: 30 Devotions for Kids, Teens, and Families
© 2025 by Beth M. Broom

Published by Crossway
        1300 Crescent Street
        Wheaton, Illinois 60187

All rights reserved. No part of this publication may be reproduced, stored in a retrieval system, or transmitted in any form by any means, electronic, mechanical, photocopy, recording, or otherwise, without the prior permission of the publisher, except as provided for by USA copyright law. Crossway® is a registered trademark in the United States of America.

Cover illustration and design: Brave Union

First printing 2025

Printed in the United States of America

Scripture quotations are from the ESV® Bible (The Holy Bible, English Standard Version®), © 2001 by Crossway, a publishing ministry of Good News Publishers. Used by permission. All rights reserved. The ESV text may not be quoted in any publication made available to the public by a Creative Commons license. The ESV may not be translated in whole or in part into any other language.

All emphases in Scripture quotations have been added by the author.

Trade paperback ISBN: 978-1-4335-9893-7
ePub ISBN: 978-1-4335-9895-1
PDF ISBN: 978-1-4335-9894-4

Library of Congress Control Number: 2025937494

Crossway is a publishing ministry of Good News Publishers.

VP		34	33	32	31	30	29	28	27	26	25
15	14	13	12	11	10	9	8	7	6	5	4	3	2	1

To Sarah, Levi, and Elijah.
I am inspired every day by your wisdom, joy, and courage.
Thank you for being three of my greatest teachers.

Contents

Series Preface *xi*
Introduction *1*

QUESTION 1
What Is Suffering?

Day 1 Everyone Suffers *5*
Day 2 God's Design *8*
Day 3 God's Rescue Plan *11*

QUESTION 2
Why Do We Suffer?

Day 4 Consequences for Sin *15*
Day 5 Pain Caused by Others *18*
Day 6 A Fallen World *21*

QUESTION 3
If God Is Good, Why Does He Let Bad Things Happen?

Day 7 Our Deepest Problem *25*
Day 8 The Devil's Limited Power *28*
Day 9 Good Things Coming *31*

QUESTION 4
Do Christians Suffer Less Than Non-Christians?

Day 10   The Just and the Unjust   35

Day 11   The Advantage of a Helper   38

Day 12   A Strong Confidence   41

QUESTION 5
When Christians Suffer, Is It Punishment?

Day 13   What We Deserve   45

Day 14   God's Plan to Grow Us   48

Day 15   Glorifying God in Suffering   51

QUESTION 6
How Does God Help Me When I'm Suffering?

Day 16   The Shade Tree   55

Day 17   Power and Protection   58

Day 18   A Wonderful Guide   61

QUESTION 7
How Should Christians Respond to Suffering?

Day 19   God's Listening Ear   65

Day 20   The Body of Christ   68

Day 21   Our Inheritance   71

QUESTION 8
What If God Doesn't Answer My Prayer for Suffering to Stop?

Day 22   Waiting for an Answer   75

Day 23   Jesus the Overcomer   78
Day 24   Purpose in the Pain   81

QUESTION 9
What Gives Someone Hope When Bad Things Keep Happening?

Day 25   The Greatest Treasure   85
Day 26   God's Powerful Love   88
Day 27   Unseen Hope   91

QUESTION 10
How Can I Help Someone Else Who Is Suffering?

Day 28   The Light of God's Love   95
Day 29   God Shows Us How   98
Day 30   Keep Going to the End   101

Key Words About Pain and Suffering   105
10 Questions About Pain and Suffering (with Answers)   109

Series Preface

Jesus loved questions.

If you open your Bible and read Matthew, Mark, Luke, and John (the Gospels), you can count over three hundred places where Jesus asked questions and over one hundred times where he answered questions.

So if you bring questions to Jesus, you've come to the right place. The Lord invites all of us to pursue him with our questions, and he will answer. "For everyone who asks receives, and the one who seeks finds, and to the one who knocks it will be opened" (Matt. 7:8).

You may have tons of questions, but the ten questions in this book will get you started. The *answers* to those ten questions are given in three daily devotional readings—three days for each question. These readings take you to the Bible, the word of God, where you can find answers to your questions. And these answers are all listed at the end of the book.

You can use this book however you like. You can skip straight to the list at the end. Or you can devour all thirty devotional readings at once, though it might take a few hours. You can read through all ten questions in order—one reading per day. Or your family could read one devotion together, perhaps at breakfast before the day or in the evening after dinner.

Find a way that works for you. But what's most important is that you listen to God's word. Whatever question is on your mind, let Jesus provide the answer through his word. If you're going to find, you must seek.

Ask him, and he will answer.

Champ Thornton

Introduction

Not everyone wants to read a book about pain and suffering. I don't know your reason for reading this book. But I'm very glad you picked it up. Usually when people read a book like this, something sad or scary has happened. They want help to understand that sad or scary thing. They want someone to show them how to get through it.

Maybe that's you. Or maybe you just want to learn what the Bible has to say about pain and suffering. That's a good thing to learn, because everyone suffers. At some point in your life, you will need help understanding suffering. You will need God's help. And you will need other people's help.

In this book we'll learn what the Bible teaches us about suffering. We'll answer questions like:

- Why do we suffer?
- If God is good, why does he let bad things happen?
- When Christians suffer, is it punishment?

We'll also talk about what we should do when we are in pain. Here are some questions we'll answer:

- How does God help me when I'm suffering?
- How should Christians respond to suffering?

- What gives someone help when bad things keep happening?

In this book we'll talk about difficult things. But you will learn to know God better. You will learn that he is full of love and kindness. You'll learn that he wants to listen and come close to you when you suffer (Pss. 55:16–17; 121:5–6). And you will find that you can have hope even when life is hard.

Question 1

What Is Suffering?

DAY 1

Everyone Suffers

Have you ever broken a bone? Maybe you've been really sick. Or maybe you have trouble finishing your schoolwork. These are all painful things that can happen to us.

Suffering can be something that happens to your body, like breaking a bone. You can also suffer in your emotions or thoughts, like when a friend says something bad about you that's not true. And sometimes suffering is really big and lasts a long time. Other times you feel better after just a day.

But here's something about suffering that's always true: Everyone deals with painful things in life. Suffering is, for now, part of what it means to be human. No person has ever experienced only good things. Everyone knows what it's like to hurt.

So, when you're suffering, what can you do to feel better? Sometimes people try to ignore their pain. They pretend it's no big deal. They think if they push down their pain, it will stop. Can you tell what's wrong about this idea? Have you ever shaken a bottle of soda? The pressure builds up pretty fast. Then you open the bottle, and soda sprays everywhere. It's the same with suffering. Ignoring or hiding our pain creates pressure inside us. That pressure can sometimes cause other problems in life. Did you know that God says it's good to talk out loud to someone who can comfort you?

> **Suffering**
>
> The state of experiencing pain or distress.

Let's look at an example in the Bible. In 1 Samuel 18 and 19, David was almost killed by someone he thought was a friend. David expressed his pain in these words:

> My heart is in anguish within me;
> > the terrors of death have fallen upon me.
> Fear and trembling come upon me,
> > and horror overwhelms me. (Ps. 55:4–5)

David was sad, afraid, and angry that his friend had hurt him. He didn't pretend everything was fine. He talked to God, and he asked God to comfort him.

> Evening and morning and at noon
> > I utter my complaint and moan,
> > and he hears my voice. (Ps. 55:17)

You can't keep away from suffering, but you can talk about it. You can talk with someone you love, and you can talk with God. This does not always make the pain stop. Yet you can receive care from someone who loves you. And that's a good feeling—like being wrapped up in a warm blanket during a snowstorm.

What is suffering? ***Suffering is the experience of pain that everyone feels.***

PRAYER

Dear God, I want to talk with you when I am suffering. I know you hear me. Thank you for listening to my problems. Please comfort me when I am in pain.

REFLECT

Who do you turn to when you are in pain? How does it feel to have someone care for you? On a separate page, you can write or draw a picture about how it feels to be comforted.

DAY 2

God's Design

Suffering didn't always exist in the world. There was a time when nothing bad ever happened. No one was sick or sad or hopeless. We see this world in Genesis 1 and 2. God made the world, and he called it good. The sky, the ocean, the animals, and the plants were all very good creations. Imagine what it must have been like to live on earth with no weeds or spider bites or algebra tests.

Then God created people. People are a special kind of this very-good creation; we are made in God's image. He gives us special work to do on earth: "Then God said, 'Let us make man in our image, after our likeness. And let them have dominion over the fish of the sea and over the birds of the heavens and over the livestock and over all the earth and over every creeping thing that creeps on the earth'" (Gen. 1:26).

But what about suffering? When God created the world, pain and sadness were not part of his universe. He wanted Adam and Eve to live in the garden of Eden with each other and with himself. He gave them instructions for taking care of the earth. He was with them in the garden. He gave them his wisdom and love.

But when Adam and Eve sinned for the first time, suffering came into the world (Gen. 2:17; Rom. 5:12; 8:18–22). Adam and Eve hid from God because they were afraid. They knew the pain of guilt and shame. Then the earth started making weeds and thorns. Now work was painful. And relationships suffered too. Adam and Eve felt angry with each other for the first time.

> **Sin**
> Doing wrong in disobedience to God.

Sin always causes suffering. You have probably seen this in your own life. When you disobey your parents, you might be grounded from something you enjoy. If someone else sins by hitting you, your body suffers a bruise. When someone makes fun of you, you feel sad, angry, or lonely. Suffering is an effect of sin.

But here is something really important: God hates sin, and God also hates suffering.

God did not enjoy sending Adam and Eve out of the garden. His plan for his people will ultimately remove all pain and suffering. But to help their pains of shame in the present moment, God gave Adam and Eve a gift. They were ashamed because they realized they were naked, so God gave them clothes to wear (Gen. 3:21). God was doing more than keeping them warm. He was providing a way for people to go out and survive in the world. He wanted them to keep living even though they were suffering. And even though they could not live in the beautiful garden anymore, God was still with them. He did not punish their sin by leaving them alone.

So what is suffering? *Suffering is the experience of pain that everyone feels. God did not design us to suffer, but sin caused suffering to enter the world.*

PRAYER

God, I am grateful that you made everything good, including me. Thank you for never leaving me even though I am a sinner. Please help me trust you more.

REFLECT

Do you think of God as a loving Father who wants to have a relationship with you? Think and talk about this with someone you love.

DAY 3
God's Rescue Plan

God hates suffering. But he also understands it. He does not stand far off and simply watch it happen to us. Psalm 23:4 says:

Even though I walk through the valley of the shadow of death,
    I will fear no evil,
for you are with me.

When we suffer, God comes close.

We see this in many Bible stories. Joseph was thrown in prison, and God was with him (Gen. 39:23). When the Israelites were slaves in Egypt, God heard their cries for help (Ex. 2:23–25). One of my favorite stories in the Bible is the account of Shadrach, Meshach, and Abednego in Daniel 3. These three men refused to bow down to King Nebuchadnezzar's statue. So he threw them in a furnace of fire. Yet God saved them. The three men did not burn. And guess what else happened? People could see a fourth person walking around in the fire with them. Many Bible experts believe this fourth person was the Lord himself. God was with them in the fire.

God's people suffered a lot in the Old Testament. Yet God always promised to be near to them when they cried out to him. He never failed them or left them alone. The Bible has many names for God, and one of my favorites is *Immanuel*. This word

> **Immanuel**
> One of the names given to Jesus; it means "God with us."

means "God with us." Isaiah 7:14 says, "The Lord himself will give you a sign. Behold, the virgin shall conceive and bear a son, and shall call his name Immanuel." This verse is written again in Matthew 1:23 to describe the birth of Jesus. It's amazing to me that God shared his great plan to send Jesus into the world hundreds of years before it happened. He wanted people to have hope that someone was coming to rescue them.

When Jesus came to this earth, he became one of us (Phil. 2:7–8). This means he suffered in the same ways you do (Heb. 4:15). It also means Jesus understands our pain. Why? Because he has had the same kind of pain. And he comforts us in our suffering. He reminds us that God is near (2 Cor. 1:3–5). He also suffered the greatest kind of pain so that we could be adopted into God's family. He died in our place because he loves us: "For God so loved the world, that he gave his only Son, that whoever believes in him should not perish but have eternal life" (John 3:16).

The good news declares that suffering has an end date. When we see Jesus face to face, all suffering will end. And while we live on this earth, we have a friend in Jesus. He sees our suffering, and he is with us.

So what is suffering? *Suffering is the experience of pain that everyone feels, because sin caused suffering to enter the world. But suffering doesn't last forever for Christians because God sent his Son into the world to suffer with us and rescue us.*

PRAYER

Dear Father, thank you for sending Jesus into the world to be one of us and to die for us. Thank you for understanding my pain. Please be with me and help me to depend on you when I suffer.

REFLECT

Do you believe that Jesus is Lord? Have you given your life to him? He invites you to become part of his family.

Question 2

Why Do We Suffer?

DAY 4

Consequences for Sin

When Adam and Eve sinned in the garden of Eden, God let them experience consequences. They had to leave their home in the garden, and that caused pain and suffering. You get it, right? When you mess up, you deal with consequences. Maybe you forgot to clean your room, and then you didn't get to go to a friend's house. Or maybe you were grounded from your favorite video game because you didn't do your homework.

The Bible is full of people who suffered consequences because of their sin. The Israelites had to wander in the wilderness for forty years because they refused to obey God (Num. 14:20–24). Jonah was swallowed up by a huge fish because he didn't want to follow God's plan (Jonah 1:7–17).

Galatians 6:7 says, "Do not be deceived: God is not mocked, for whatever one sows, that will he also reap." This is a farming example. It means that if you sow (or plant) sin in life, that seed of sin will reap (or create) a consequence.

Consequences are not fun, but we have them so we will learn. They are supposed to be a bit painful. That's what helps us remember to obey next time. Not all suffering happens because you did something bad, but sin usually causes painful consequences. We don't have to be glad about being disciplined. But we can remember that God gives us consequences because he loves us.

> **Consequence**
> The result of a sinful or harmful action.

Think about it like this: If your dog runs out into the street, you will do something to make sure he doesn't get run over by a car. You might yell at him. You might even put a training collar on him. You don't do this to be mean. You want to teach him, with a little pain, that the street is dangerous and could bring bigger pain. This is what God does when he disciplines us. He knows that sin is dangerous, and he wants us to know it too.

So why do we suffer? *Sometimes we suffer as a consequence of our sin.*

PRAYER

Dear God, please help me remember that the consequences for my sin teach me to obey. Thank you for sending Jesus to die for my sin. Please forgive my sin and keep showing me how to follow you.

REFLECT

Can you remember a time when you sinned and felt the consequences? How did you respond? Next time you have a consequence, remember that consequences help you to grow.

DAY 5
Pain Caused by Others

We can't have a world full of sinners and not have a world where we hurt each other. Let's say you and I are friends. One day I come to school in a very bad mood. You ask if I want to hang out after school. I yell, "Leave me alone! I don't even like you." Of course you'd be surprised. Your feelings would be hurt. Even if I didn't mean it, you'd still feel sad. Maybe you'd even be angry.

This is an example of how someone else's sin can cause suffering. You didn't do anything to deserve what I said, but you're still hurt by it. In the Bible, David was hurt by other people, when he didn't do anything wrong. Listen to Psalm 56:1:

Be gracious to me, O God, for man tramples on me;
    all day long an attacker oppresses me.

The person who was hurting David was doing it on purpose. Someone was treating him so badly that he felt like he was being smashed down into the dirt. This is what it means to be *oppressed*.

Have you ever felt like this? We all feel sad and angry when someone else does something that hurts us. And sometimes we experience consequences when someone hurts us. Sometimes the pain inside us leads to other bad things. If I yell at you, then you might not feel good about being friends with me. Our friendship might end. That's a consequence you wouldn't deserve.

If someone hurts you over and over, you might start to wonder if you did something to cause it. When other people hurt us, it's hard to understand the reason. It can be easy to blame ourselves. But we are not in charge of other people's actions or feelings. It's not our fault when someone else sins.

> **Oppress**
> To cause someone else to feel pain or distress.

Jesus is the best example of someone who experienced consequences because of someone else's sin. Imagine never doing anything wrong and still being killed. Jesus was treated like he was the worst person on earth. He took punishment even though he didn't deserve it. Yet he is the perfect Savior and friend to us. As our Savior, he forgives our sin. And as our friend, he is with us when we suffer.

So why do we suffer? *Sometimes we suffer as a consequence of our sin, and sometimes we suffer when other people sin.*

PRAYER

Dear Lord, it really hurts when someone sins against me. I am glad you understand. I need you to be my friend. Please give me strength and comfort when people hurt me.

REFLECT

Has someone ever hurt you and caused you to suffer? Who do you talk to when this happens? Next time someone hurts you, share your sadness with God and ask him to come near to you.

DAY 6
A Fallen World

Before Adam and Eve sinned, the world was very good. After they sinned, the world changed. Here is what God said to Adam after he sinned:

> Because you have listened to the voice of your wife
> and have eaten of the tree
> of which I commanded you,
> 'You shall not eat of it,'
> cursed is the ground because of you;
> in pain you shall eat of it all the days of your life;
> thorns and thistles it shall bring forth for you;
> and you shall eat the plants of the field.
> By the sweat of your face
> you shall eat bread,
> till you return to the ground,
> for out of it you were taken;
> for you are dust,
> and to dust you shall return. (Gen. 3:17–19)

After sin came into the world, thorns and thistles started coming out of the ground. Adam's work as a farmer got a lot harder. Suffering can happen because we live in a fallen world. What

> **Fallen**
>
> The state of the world after Adam and Eve sinned; a state of hardship, sin, and suffering.

does it mean to say the world is *fallen*? It means everything on earth is affected by sin. God made his creation perfect. It's still good and wonderful—yet it's also broken.

My son's friend recently fell into a thornbush while they were playing. The thorns scratched and bruised his legs. He had to stop playing and clean up the cuts, and he was in a lot of pain. Our fallen world caused him to suffer.

Do you know someone who has a disease? Have you ever broken a bone or had to get stitches? Has your town had a tornado or hurricane? These are all ways we suffer because we live in a fallen world. And here is the worst type of suffering: Genesis 3:17–19 tells us we will all die someday.

Let's remember this: God wants a relationship with us, but sin keeps us from being close to him. So he made a way for us to be made clean from our sin. He sent Jesus into the world to die in our place. We still have to live in a world where sin causes suffering. But we can be close to God and be forgiven by God (1 Pet. 3:18).

So why do we suffer? *Sometimes we suffer as a consequence of our sin, sometimes we suffer when other people sin, and sometimes we suffer because we live in a fallen world.*

PRAYER

Dear God, it's hard to live in a world where bad things happen. I don't like it, and I'm glad you don't like it either. Thank you for being with me in this fallen world. Please give me peace when I suffer because I live in a fallen world.

REFLECT

Do you feel close to God? Even though you cannot see him, you can still believe that he loves you and know that he is close to you because of the life and death of his Son, Jesus.

Question 3

If God Is Good, Why Does He Let Bad Things Happen?

DAY 7
Our Deepest Problem

The Bible tells us that everything in creation was affected by sin: "The creation was subjected to futility, not willingly, but because of him who subjected it, in hope that the creation itself will be set free from its bondage to corruption and obtain the freedom of the glory of the children of God" (Rom. 8:20–21).

God does not enjoy that we suffer. But he uses suffering in our lives as a way for us to remember something important: We are broken because of sin. We don't have hope unless God provides a way for us to be free.

When I was young, we used to play a game where one kid was in "jail" and her team had to find her and get her out. The other team was in charge of guarding the jail. I never liked being the one in jail. It was boring. I just had to sit there and wait to be rescued.

This is what the writer of Romans means when he uses the word *bondage*. It means you're being held captive with no way of escape unless someone else helps you. Romans 8:20–21 says we were in bondage to *corruption*. Corruption happens when something gets worse and worse. It's kind of like rust that grows on your bike if you leave it out in the rain. If no one steps in to fix it, that rust will destroy your bike.

Suffering reminds us that we have been captured and have no way out. When we suffer, it helps us remember that sin is like

> **Corruption**
> The process of decay because of sin, becoming worse and worse over time.

rust that ruins us. But look at the end of the verse. God allows suffering for a purpose: the hope of being set free. When we think about our suffering, we need to remember that sin will destroy us unless someone rescues us. And God has provided that rescuer: Jesus. He wants us to be free. He made a plan for our suffering to be turned into joy.

So if God is good, why does he let bad things happen? *Suffering reminds us of our deep problem of sin.*

PRAYER

Dear Father, I know that sin holds me captive. I need to be rescued. Even though I don't like to suffer, it is a good reminder that I need a Savior. Thank you for providing Jesus as the way for me to be free.

REFLECT

After reading today's devotional, what do you want to remember about suffering? Telling someone else what you are learning helps you remember it even better.

DAY 8
The Devil's Limited Power

God is the Creator of the universe. He's in charge of everything. So why can't he just make sure everyone is happy all the time? And if he really loves us, why does he let us suffer?

If you have these questions, you're not alone. One answer the Bible gives us is that the devil is hard at work. He has the power to tempt us into disobedience. He tries to get us to sin. The Bible says he wants to devour us: "Be sober-minded; be watchful. Your adversary the devil prowls around like a roaring lion, seeking someone to devour" (1 Pet. 5:8). But here's the good news: The devil's power is limited.

Let's compare it to something you can see with your eyes. Have you ever looked at a photo of the earth taken from space? You can see the earth, but you can also see the edge of the earth's atmosphere. It looks like a ring around the outside of the planet.

The devil's power is like the atmosphere around the earth. It only goes so far, and then it stops. God has given the devil a boundary, just as he has given the earth's atmosphere a boundary.

So when suffering happens, it does not mean God has lost control. It means he has given the devil some limited power to spread evil throughout the world. And because God is in control—even over the devil's limited power—we can pray to God and ask him to help us in our suffering. God has also given us weapons and armor so we can fight against the devil's power (Eph. 6:10–18). He has not left us alone. He is with us, and he gives us strength and hope in our suffering.

> **Power**
> The ability to be strong and do something to cause change.

The next time you wonder why God lets bad things happen, remember the ring of the earth's atmosphere. The devil has power, but his power has limits. Only God has ultimate power.

So if God is good, why does he let bad things happen? *Suffering reminds us of our deep problem of sin and that the world is under the devil's limited power.*

PRAYER

Dear God, thank you that you are in charge of everything. Thank you that the devil does not have all the power. Please give me strength to hope in you. Thank you for always being with me.

REFLECT

Does it help you to remember that God has more power than sin and suffering? What is a way you can try to keep remembering this when suffering happens?

DAY 9

Good Things Coming

We have learned that suffering reminds us of our sin problem. And the devil has power to lead people toward sin. If these things are true, suffering is sure to happen in the world. But does suffering have some sort of purpose in *my* life?

I heard a story about a girl who had to get water from a well every day. The well was a mile from her house. She carried a clay pot to haul the water. But there was a problem. The pot had a crack in it. So by the time she'd get back home, the pot would be only about half full. She kept having to go back and forth to get enough water. This was very frustrating. But one day she noticed tiny flowers growing along the path. It turns out the leaky pot had been watering the path so that flowers could grow. She did not like the hard work, but something good was also happening.

This is how it is with suffering. James 1:2–4 says: "Count it all joy, my brothers, when you meet trials of various kinds, for you know that the testing of your faith produces steadfastness. And let steadfastness have its full effect, that you may be perfect and complete, lacking in nothing."

James tells us that the trials we face cause us to have steadfastness. That's like when you go running every day and then notice it gets easier over time. When you keep doing something,

> **Steadfastness**
> The quality of being firm, strong, and unchanging.

you get stronger. The result of getting stronger is that you become "perfect and complete." That means mature. It doesn't mean you don't ever mess up or get tired. It means you run all the way to the finish line.

Does it seem weird that the Bible says we should "count it all joy"? Does that mean we should be glad that we suffer? No. It means that we can notice how suffering turns our hearts to God. We pray to him and ask for help. We keep believing he is good, and we have hope. And we can be glad that our suffering brings something good: a stronger faith.

So if God is good, why does he let bad things happen? *Suffering reminds us of our deep problem of sin and that the world is under the devil's limited power, but God creates good things through bad things.*

PRAYER

Dear God, I'm glad that something good can come from suffering. Thank you that you make your children's faith stronger as we keep going through suffering. Please help me to keep believing you are good.

REFLECT

Is it hard to believe that something good can come from your suffering? Take some time to think of ways you might be getting stronger as you go through hard things.

Question 4

Do Christians Suffer Less Than Non-Christians?

DAY 10

The Just and the Unjust

Have you ever heard that if you follow God and do what is right, nothing bad will happen to you? The Bible does tell us that obeying God leads to good things. But it does not promise that we won't suffer. In fact, the Bible tells us just the opposite.

In Matthew 5:45, Jesus says, "[God] makes his sun rise on the evil and on the good, and sends rain on the just and on the unjust." Jesus is saying that Christians aren't protected from harm simply because they are "just" (a "just" person is someone who acts in a way that is right and fair).

No matter the type of person you are, you will go through hard things in life. That's because you live in a world that is full of sin. Evil people will experience good things, and good people will experience evil things.

This may not seem fair to you. But think about "evil people" for a moment. When God shows good to them, it's his way of showing grace to people who don't care about him at all. Even people who do all the wrong things have happy times. Those happy times are meant to point them to God's love (even though they may not see it). And the hard things Christians experience are also meant to point them to God's love.

God does not keep bad things from happening. But he provides for us when we are hurting. He comes close to us.

> **Just**
> Behaving according to what is right and fair.

Do you need proof that Christians do not suffer less than non-Christians? Just look at some of the people in the Bible. In 2 Corinthians 11:24–28, the apostle Paul talks about lots of bad things that happened to him: He was shipwrecked, beaten, robbed, betrayed, starved, and put in prison. Some of these things happened *because* he was telling people about Jesus. And Paul is just one example.

The most important person who suffered is Jesus. When he died on the cross, he suffered more than we ever will. And he did this because he loves us. He wants us to know God. Though Christians will continue to experience suffering on this earth, we can know that Jesus's suffering made a way for our suffering to end someday—in heaven and in the new heaven and new earth.

So do Christians have less suffering than non-Christians? *Christians do not suffer less than non-Christians because all humans experience both good and evil.*

PRAYER

Dear Lord, I want to be protected from bad things, but I know our world is full of sin. Please help me trust you when bad things happen. Please come close to me when I am suffering.

REFLECT

What do you wish would happen when you suffer? Share your desires with God and ask him to help you trust him with things that are hard.

DAY 11
The Advantage of a Helper

Even though Christians sometimes suffer as much as non-Christians, we have an advantage in our suffering. An *advantage* is something that helps you win. Let's say you and I are playing a game using Nerf guns. I have a small gun that holds six Nerf darts. You have a Nerf Blaster with a rotating barrel (which holds fifteen darts). We would say that you have an advantage—there's a good chance you will beat me.

Of course Nerf wars are just fun and games; the battle we fight every day is a spiritual one. So what is our advantage as Christians? We have the Holy Spirit. When Jesus was preparing to die for our sins and then go to heaven, he said this to his disciples:

> The Helper, the Holy Spirit, whom the Father will send in my name, he will teach you all things and bring to your remembrance all that I have said to you. Peace I leave with you; my peace I give to you. Not as the world gives do I give to you. Let not your hearts be troubled, neither let them be afraid. (John 14:26–27)

Jesus knew he could not be with all of us at once. So he put the Holy Spirit inside every Christian. The Holy Spirit's job is to comfort us, teach us, correct us, and help us serve the church

(John 16:7–15; Rom. 12:3–8; 1 Cor. 12:4–11). This is great news. We don't have to figure out how to live a good life by ourselves. The Holy Spirit is our guide.

> **Helper**
> Someone who supports someone else.

The Holy Spirit is not a person we can physically see, standing in front of us. So it can be hard to know how to listen to him. But God has given us ways to listen to him. The most important way is through the Bible. When we read it, we are hearing God's voice.

We can also be encouraged by the Holy Spirit through God's people. Has someone ever prayed for you or encouraged you? God's Spirit was using that person to show you his love. And when we pray, we are not just talking. We are also listening to God. We are having a conversation with him. The next time you pray, ask God to respond to you. Maybe he will remind you of a verse in the Bible. Or maybe you will simply feel comforted. These are ways the Holy Spirit encourages us.

So do Christians have less suffering than non-Christians? *Christians do not suffer less than non-Christians because all humans experience both good and evil, but Christians have a Helper in our suffering.*

PRAYER

Dear Lord, please help me to listen to you when I read my Bible. Please encourage me when other people pray for me and help me.

REFLECT

Do you ever ask God to talk back to you? Next time someone encourages you or you read the Bible, notice how God might be talking through other people and his word.

DAY 12

A Strong Confidence

Everyone hopes for good things to happen. We hope for a certain birthday present, or we hope for a fun vacation. Christians have a certain kind of hope. It's not the same as a wish for something—it's a strong confidence that God keeps his promises.

Listen to Paul's words in Romans 5:1–5:

> Since we have been justified by faith, we have peace with God through our Lord Jesus Christ. Through him we have also obtained access by faith into this grace in which we stand, and we rejoice in hope of the glory of God. Not only that, but we rejoice in our sufferings, knowing that suffering produces endurance, and endurance produces character, and character produces hope, and hope does not put us to shame, because God's love has been poured into our hearts through the Holy Spirit who has been given to us.

Since God has saved us, we now have his grace. This means God forgives our sin. He welcomes us into his family. The "hope of the glory of God" is the confidence God gives us that we belong to him. And someday we will be with him in heaven. So even though our suffering might not be less than what non-Christians experience, we have something to look forward to.

> **Hope**
> A feeling of strong confidence in a person or circumstance.

But then Paul says something that may seem strange. He says we rejoice in our suffering. Does this mean we should be happy that we suffer? No, it means we can have hope and rejoice even as we suffer and keep following God. We believe we are getting stronger and closer to God.

Look back at the Bible verses above. Can you see three things that happen when we suffer as Christians? *Suffering produces endurance*, which means we get stronger. *Endurance produces character*, which means we think and act more like Jesus. And *character produces hope*, which means we have more and more confidence that God keeps his promises.

Think about something you are learning, like playing the piano or shooting a basketball. It's hard work. But the more you do it, the better you get. And the better you get, the more confidence you have. The same is true of our faith, except in addition to our "practicing" (learning to suffer) we also have the Holy Spirit helping us. That's like having the best pianist playing with you or a pro basketball player lifting you up to dunk the basketball!

So do Christians have less suffering than non-Christians? *Christians do not suffer less than non-Christians because all humans experience both good and evil, but Christians have a Helper and a strong hope in our suffering.*

PRAYER

Dear Father, I am glad that we can have hope when we suffer. Please help me to keep following you and listening to the Holy Spirit. Make me stronger and closer to you when life is hard.

REFLECT

Do you feel hopeful that God keeps his promises? Do you have confidence in him? Ask him to keep helping your hope to grow.

Question 5

When Christians Suffer, Is It Punishment?

DAY 13

What We Deserve

Back in question 2 we talked about how sometimes we suffer because we sin. Let's go a little further and talk about punishment.

Have you ever done a job for money? Let's say you mow your neighbors' lawn for twenty dollars. They give you the money after you have finished mowing. You earned a *wage*, which is money paid to you for doing the job.

Romans 6:23 says, "The wages of sin is death." A wage is something you earn. And because we are all sinners, we all earn the punishment of death. Apart from someone taking that punishment away, there is no way to avoid receiving that "wage" we've earned.

But let's read the rest of Romans 6:23: "The wages of sin is death, *but the free gift of God is eternal life in Christ Jesus our Lord.*" Thank God for the second half of that verse! We all deserve the punishment of death because of our sin. But there's a solution. Those who trust Jesus as Savior have eternal life instead of death. Because of Jesus, we do not have to get the punishment, the "wages," we deserve.

God gave the punishment we deserved to Jesus instead of us. Isn't that amazing? He loved us so much that he sent his perfect Son into the world. Listen to the words of Isaiah 53:5:

> He was pierced for our transgressions;
>> he was crushed for our iniquities;
> upon him was the chastisement that brought us peace,
>> and with his wounds we are healed.

Jesus took our *transgressions* and our *iniquities*. These are big words to describe sin. And *chastisement* is a big word to describe punishment.

So this means that when Christians sin, they aren't being punished by God. The good news of the gospel is that he was willing to give the punishment we deserved to Jesus so he could be close to us.

So when Christians suffer, is it punishment? *No. For anyone who believes in him, Jesus has taken the punishment that sinners deserve.*

> **Punishment**
> The penalty for doing something wrong.

PRAYER

Dear Lord, thank you that you loved me enough to give Jesus the punishment I deserve. That means I do not have to be separated from you. Please forgive my sin and draw me close to you.

REFLECT

Have you ever thought about the punishment you deserve because of sin? Do you believe Jesus took your punishment in order to save you?

DAY 14
God's Plan to Grow Us

Good parents discipline their kids when they sin, but they don't do it to be mean. They want to teach their children to make better choices. Punishment is giving a penalty for sin, but *discipline* is meant to move us back to the right path.

I used to teach math to third graders. Every day, we practiced the multiplication tables. My students didn't like it very much. Some of them said it was boring and hard. But after doing this every day for about a month, the kids knew the answers without having to think about them. They had been disciplined to learn their math facts.

Discipline is about being shaped (sometimes by something difficult) so we will grow. Hebrews 12:11 says, "For the moment all discipline seems painful rather than pleasant, but later it yields the peaceful fruit of righteousness to those who have been trained by it." Hebrews 12 also says that when God disciplines us, he is treating us like sons (12:7). He loves us so much that he wants us to be strong and wise. We cannot be strong and wise without practice or discipline.

God uses our suffering to help us get stronger and wiser. When we receive God's discipline, we get "the peaceful fruit of righteousness." Righteousness is the result of God's discipline. We look more like Jesus, and we live in a way that is wise.

Now here's something important: Sometimes, even when you haven't sinned, you might think God is punishing you. Even as a Christian, you sometimes might feel like you're a bad person. So when bad things happen, you might feel like you deserve it. This is not how God works.

> **Discipline**
> The practice of training people to obey and make wise choices.

It's never the Lord's ultimate plan to push his children down or make us feel terrible about ourselves. He always wants us to be near to him and keep growing. So if you feel like a terrible person, remember that this is not the way God sees you. He loves you and is shaping your life.

So when Christians suffer, is it punishment? *No. For anyone who believes in him, Jesus has taken the punishment that sinners deserve; God wants to grow us, not punish us.*

PRAYER

Dear God, it's not fun to be disciplined for my sin. But thank you for wanting me to grow and learn. Please help me to know that you discipline me so I will be stronger and wiser.

REFLECT

Does it ever feel like God is punishing you by making you suffer? When you feel like this, remember that he loves his children. He works hard to help keep us on the right path.

DAY 15

Glorifying God in Suffering

When bad things happen, we want to know why. This is how our brains naturally work. As we talked about in the previous day's reading, sometimes we might think a bad thing happened because we deserved it. Sometimes we can think a bad thing happened because God doesn't care about us. And at other times, we just want to know whose fault it is.

There's a Bible story about this in John 9:1–7. Jesus and his disciples were going from town to town preaching the gospel and healing people. One day they walked past a man who had been blind since he was born. "His disciples asked him, 'Rabbi, who sinned, this man or his parents, that he was born blind?' Jesus answered, 'It was not that this man sinned, or his parents, but that the works of God might be displayed in him'" (9:2–3). Guess what Jesus did after this? He spit on the ground and made mud. He rubbed the mud on the man's eyes, and the man was able to see!

This story shows us that God is at work through bad things that happen. The blind man had spent his whole life not being able to see. But God had a purpose in this hardship: When Jesus healed him, everyone around them saw God's miracle. Everyone could see God's love and power to heal. Sometimes I wonder if the blind man was sad that he had not been healed

> **Glorify**
> To celebrate and describe someone as wonderful and worthy.

sooner. He probably wished he had never been blind. But at this moment, I also think he was happy. Even though he had suffered a lot, now he was free and ready to give his life to Jesus. Other bad things in his life did not go away. But now he had something new to give him joy.

God is *glorified* when he uses our suffering to help us grow. This means we see how good he is, and we praise him. We see his power, his grace, and his faithfulness. Sometimes it's hard to see these things because of our pain. But we can look up and notice that he loves us. We can choose to believe that he is doing something good even when we cannot see it.

So when Christians suffer, is it punishment? *No. For anyone who believes in him, Jesus has taken the punishment that sinners deserve; God wants to grow us, not punish us, and his glory is shown as he helps and heals us.*

PRAYER

Dear God, I want to be able to see that you are good and faithful through my suffering. When I think maybe you are not good, please remind me of the truth.

REFLECT

Do you believe that God is glorified when we suffer, and does that help you grow closer to him? If this is hard for you, you're not alone. It's good to ask God to help you believe and see his way more clearly.

Question 6

How Does God Help Me When I'm Suffering?

DAY 16
The Shade Tree

Have you ever had a friend who was in trouble or in pain? When something scary or sad happens to someone we care about, we don't always know how to help. Sometimes we ignore the problem or try to make it seem small. Sometimes we want to run away.

But God never runs away when we suffer. He never pretends our problems are small. In fact, he invites us to bring our suffering to him. When we are brokenhearted or crushed in spirit, we can count on him.

Now as we've said before, God doesn't always take away the hard thing that's happening. But he gives us a great gift that helps our pain: He gives us himself. He provides comfort and strength so that we can keep going.

Psalm 121:5–6 paints a beautiful word picture. It says that God is like a shade tree:

The Lord is your keeper;
>   the Lord is your shade on your right hand.
The sun shall not strike you by day,
>   nor the moon by night.

Have you ever been outside with no shade in the summer? If you're out too long, it can be unbearable. This passage calls

> **Keeper**
> A person who manages or looks after something or someone.

God our *keeper*. That means he's in charge as our protector. He watches over us and takes care of us. A shade tree can help only if you are standing under it. When we come under God's protection, he provides us with shelter. The sun still might beat down, but he is our shade where we find protection.

God doesn't turn his back on us. He doesn't leave us alone in the hot summer sun. He cares. He provides for us and invites us to come to him when we suffer. Let's keep that picture in mind when we think of what God does when we are suffering.

So how does God help me when I'm suffering? *God comes near.*

PRAYER

Dear Lord, thank you for inviting me to come to you when I am suffering. Thank you for rescuing and providing for me. Please remind me that you are good and that I can trust you.

REFLECT

Think about the image of a shade tree. Imagine yourself under that tree. Now imagine that God is that tree. Say a prayer of thanks to God for being your shade when suffering happens.

DAY 17

Power and Protection

It's good to know that God is near to us when we suffer. He listens to us and comforts us. But we also want to know that God is doing something to help us get through the hard times.

David had the same thoughts:

Blessed be the LORD!
    For he has heard the voice of my pleas for mercy.
The LORD is my strength and my shield;
    in him my heart trusts, and I am helped;
my heart exults,
    and with my song I give thanks to him. (Ps. 28:6–7)

David was grateful that God heard his voice when he cried out for help. But David was also grateful for something else. He called God his *strength* and his *shield.* Let's think about those two words.

Have you ever seen TV characters who wore armor when they fought a battle? The purpose of armor is to protect the body. Without it, people usually don't win. When David called God his *shield*, he meant that God protected him. David was not alone in the battle. God shielded him.

And when David called God his *strength*, he meant that God helped him powerfully fight against his enemies. As we've said before, David had a lot of enemies. Most of them hated him for bad reasons. So he needed a lot of strength, and God gave it to him. David knew he could not win without God's help. He praised God for helping him. He also trusted God to keep his promises to protect and help him.

> **Protection**
> Keeping someone safe from harm or danger.

You've probably never worn real armor. You might never have to fight in an actual battle. But you need power and protection every day. You need God to be your strength and shield. He is eager to help you in whatever hard things you face.

So how does God help me when I'm suffering? *God comes near, and he gives strength and protection.*

PRAYER

Dear Father, thank you that you draw near to me in hard times. I need you to give me strength and protection. Please help me trust you to keep your promises. Thank you for being faithful.

REFLECT

How do we gain strength to get through suffering? What makes God's power real to us? We experience God's strength when we read his word, pray, and worship him with other people. What are some ways you can keep getting stronger?

DAY 18

A Wonderful Guide

Have you ever gotten lost at a zoo or an amusement park? Maybe your family has been lost while driving somewhere new. It can be confusing and scary when you don't know which way to go. What do you need most when you get lost? You need a guide to help you get back on track.

When I was five years old, I got lost at a huge amusement park with lots of rides and games. I remember feeling very frightened. I stood still and cried. Finally, a police officer came over and talked to me. He asked me some questions and helped me find my parents. He was my guide when I was lost.

Life can be confusing and scary. And amid suffering, the confusion and fear can be even bigger. There's a word for knowing which way to go in such times: *wisdom*. Wisdom is the ability to make good decisions, and it comes from God. The Bible tells us that God is the author of wisdom. He invented it. So he always knows the best thing to do.

And here's the great news: God wants to give us wisdom. He doesn't like it when we are confused or scared. He is a wonderful guide, and he can show us the way. James 1:5 says, "If any of you lacks wisdom, let him ask God, who gives generously to all without reproach, and it will be given to him."

> **Wisdom**
> The quality of having experience, knowledge, and good judgment.

All we have to do is ask God, and he shares his wisdom with us. In fact, God is *generous*. He gives us more wisdom than we even ask for. James also says God gives *without reproach*. This means God is not disappointed in us when we ask for wisdom. He knows we need it, and he is eager to provide.

You can ask God for wisdom when you feel confused or scared. Ask him to guide you and show you which way to go. Then it's important to listen to God. How can we do that? We can read the Bible. We can also receive wisdom by talking with another Christian who is wise. We can listen to our pastors, ministers, and parents. These are all ways God shares wisdom with us.

So how does God help me when I'm suffering? *God comes near, and he gives strength, protection, and wisdom.*

PRAYER

Dear Lord, thank you for being generous. Please give me wisdom when I don't know which way to go. Please help me listen to you by reading the Bible and listening to people who are wise.

REFLECT

Is there anything happening in your life right now that is confusing or scary? Have you asked God for wisdom? You can ask him now and then talk with someone who is wise. You can thank God for being generous.

Question 7

How Should Christians Respond to Suffering?

DAY 19
God's Listening Ear

Most kids have some kind of toy or blanket to give them comfort when they are sad or scared. Do you have something like that? You probably feel safer when you have it with you.

It's important to be comforted when we are in pain. We all need someone to encourage us and listen to us. Hopefully you have someone in your life who gives you comfort. Did you know that God also wants to fill that role in your life? By his Holy Spirit, God offers comfort to Christians as they bring their burdens to him.

We've talked about David a lot in this book. He was a king who had many enemies. Often he was in danger because people were chasing him. And sometimes he didn't have anybody to turn to for comfort. But he always knew he could turn to God. Listen to these words in Psalm 55:16–17:

> I call to God,
>   and the LORD will save me.
> Evening and morning and at noon
>   I utter my complaint and moan,
>   and he hears my voice.

In his suffering, David called out to God. And he didn't just call out one time. Verse 16 says he called out all day long! He kept

> **Complaint**
>
> A statement that a situation is difficult or painful.

telling God his complaint, the thing he was upset about. And God heard his voice. When Christians suffer, the first thing they should do is talk to God. Why? Because God listens. He doesn't turn us away. He gives us his Holy Spirit to comfort us in our pain.

Jesus set an example for us. He too talked to God when he was suffering. When he knew he was about to be killed, he talked with God all night. He asked for comfort and help. And even though God didn't stop people from killing Jesus, he kept turning to God in his suffering. We learn in Hebrews 4:15 that Jesus understands our suffering. This means he's the greatest listener ever. He knows what it's like to suffer. He has compassion on us. And he doesn't get tired of hearing about our pain.

So how should Christians respond to suffering? *Through prayer, we seek comfort from God.*

PRAYER

Dear God, thank you for comforting me when I am in pain. I want to remember to talk to you when I suffer. I want to be honest with you and accept your comfort.

REFLECT

Have you ever told God about the things you are feeling? You might want to write down your prayer like David did, and then say it out loud. God wants to hear from you, and he will keep listening.

DAY 20

The Body of Christ

We know that God wants to listen to us and comfort us in our suffering. But we also know that God is not a person with a body. He does not hug us or talk to us directly in conversation. So he gave us a special gift to help us feel his comfort. He gave us other people.

Think back to a time you were really scared. Now think about who helped you. Was there someone close by who talked with you and hugged you? That probably made you feel a lot better. Without other people to comfort us, we would feel alone and probably more afraid.

God talks about his people in a special way. He calls them the "body of Christ." He uses this picture to help us understand how we are supposed to live together. Your body is an amazing creation. All the muscles and veins and bones work together to help you move around. God made his church like a body. No part works by itself. Instead, all the parts of the body work together.

Think of it like this. If you stub your toe, your whole leg feels it. You might have trouble thinking because of the pain. The same is true for the body of Christ. First Corinthians 12:26 says, "If one member suffers, all suffer together; if one member is honored, all rejoice together." In other words, we are supposed to share our suffering and joy with other people.

Other people can help carry our suffering. Galatians 6:2 says, "Bear one another's burdens, and so fulfill the law of Christ." If you are carrying a heavy burden, God wants someone else to help you. It might be hard to tell someone about your struggle, but it's even harder to suffer alone.

So how should Christians respond to suffering? *Through prayer, we seek comfort from God and help from other people.*

> **Burden**
> A heavy load that someone carries.

PRAYER

Dear God, thank you for giving me the gift of people who can help me when I suffer. Give me courage to talk with someone when I need help.

REFLECT

Have you ever told someone how you felt when you were in pain? What did that feel like? If it was someone you trust, it probably felt good. Ask God to give you courage to be honest about your feelings.

DAY 21

Our Inheritance

In question 4 we talked about how we can have hope in our suffering because we belong to Jesus. Jesus gives us confidence through the Holy Spirit, who lives in us. And we can respond to our suffering by putting our hope into action.

Let's see how the Holy Spirit offers us hope:

> The Spirit himself bears witness with our spirit that we are children of God, and if children, then heirs—heirs of God and fellow heirs with Christ, provided we suffer with him in order that we may also be glorified with him. For I consider that the sufferings of this present time are not worth comparing with the glory that is to be revealed to us. (Rom. 8:16–18)

The Holy Spirit reminds us that we are God's children. If we are his children, that means we are also *heirs*. This word means we will inherit something. This doesn't always happen today, but during Bible times people regularly gave gifts to their children when they died. These gifts were the children's inheritance. Sometimes parents gave a house or money to their children. An inheritance is a gift that is promised to beloved children.

The Bible tells us that we have an inheritance as God's children. What is our inheritance? Heaven! Romans 8:16–18 tells us that we

> **Inheritance**
> A gift you receive after a loved one's death.

are going to suffer in this life. But our suffering can't even compare to the joy and goodness we will have someday in heaven. It doesn't mean our suffering is tiny—it just means heaven is huge! It's a gift that is so much bigger than our pain.

When Christians suffer, they respond by reminding themselves that an inheritance is coming. Someday everything that's bad will end. God will make everything right. We will never cry again. This is great news, and when we're suffering, we need to remember our glorious future.

So how should Christians respond to suffering? *Through prayer, we seek comfort from God and help from other people, always holding on to the hope of heaven.*

PRAYER

Dear Father, thank you for giving an inheritance to your children. Thank you for giving us heaven. Please help me to remember and have hope when I am suffering.

REFLECT

What do you think about heaven? Did you know that it's an inheritance for God's children? On a separate page, you can draw a picture or write about heaven and think about what it will be like.

Question 8

What If God Doesn't Answer My Prayer for Suffering to Stop?

DAY 22

Waiting for an Answer

Have you ever had to wait a long time to get something you wanted?

When I was a kid, I planned months ahead for my birthday. I made a list of the things I wanted, and I thought about who I should invite to my party. I also remember thinking it was going to take forever for my birthday to come.

It's hard enough to wait for something you're excited about. It can be even harder to wait for something painful to stop. The Bible teaches us to pray whenever we need help (James 5:13–14). But sometimes God doesn't answer our prayers quickly. And sometimes it seems like he isn't answering at all.

When King David was suffering, he felt the same way. Here are his words in Psalm 13:1:

How long, O Lord? Will you forget me forever?
    How long will you hide your face from me?

Does it surprise you to see these questions in the Bible? David was a strong and wise man. But he got frustrated when it seemed like God wasn't answering.

It makes sense to feel frustrated in our suffering. The longer we wait, the more frustrated we can get. But we can learn

> **Waiting**
>
> The action of staying where you are until something else happens.

from David. Even though he was frustrated, he still talked to God. In honest yet respectful ways, he kept asking God for what he needed. We can do the same.

Even if it takes a long time for suffering to stop, we can trust God to make everything right. He promises that he will. Ecclesiastes 3:11 says, "He has made everything beautiful in its time." This means God knows the right time for everything. He doesn't forget about us. He has good plans for us. So we keep talking to him and asking for what we need. We keep coming to him for comfort and wisdom.

So, what if God doesn't answer my prayer for suffering to stop? *You can trust God even when his plans don't make sense to you.*

PRAYER

Dear God, it's hard to wait for you to answer my prayers. Sometimes I wonder if you're listening. But I know you haven't forgotten me. Please help me keep coming to you for comfort and wisdom.

REFLECT

Think of something you had to wait a long time to get. How did it feel when you finally got it? Even though waiting is hard, we can have confidence in God's goodness. Write a prayer to God thanking him for times he has answered your prayers.

DAY 23

Jesus the Overcomer

When Jesus was on earth, he had twelve special friends, called *disciples*. These guys followed him around and learned from him. They listened to him teach and watched him perform miracles. They spent all their time with him for three years.

Then the time came when Jesus was about to be crucified. He started to tell his disciples things they didn't like. He said he would be killed. He said they would be afraid and would run away. Peter, one of Jesus's best friends, argued with Jesus. He said he would never run away (Matt. 26:35). But guess what? When Jesus was arrested, all the disciples were terrified. They all ran away (26:56).

Even though Jesus knew they would do this, he still wanted to encourage them. He wanted them to have peace. He said, "I have said these things to you, that in me you may have peace. In the world you will have tribulation. But take heart; I have overcome the world" (John 16:33).

Jesus didn't lie to the disciples. He told them they would have *tribulation*, which means they would suffer. But he also said they could *take heart*, which means to have courage. He has *overcome* the world. This means he succeeded against an enemy. The enemy is sin, and Jesus overcame this enemy by dying on the cross. And when Jesus overcame sin, he won salvation for all who believe in him.

So we can know two things at the same time. We know our prayers for suffering to end might not be answered right away, and we also know Jesus has overcome the world. Suffering is not the winner. Jesus is the winner. And his victory will last forever. In fact, the Bible tells us that someday there will be a whole new heaven and earth. When that happens, sin and suffering will no longer exist. Everything will be good and joyful.

> **Overcome**
>
> To succeed in defeating an enemy or problem.

It can be hard to focus on this truth when we are in pain. But it's the way we keep going. It's like running in a race and being able to see the finish line. Jesus finished the race and won, and we can keep running to him because he has overcome.

So, what if God doesn't answer my prayer for suffering to stop? *You can trust God even when his plans don't make sense to you, knowing that he sent Jesus to save you and give you peace.*

PRAYER

Dear Lord, I want to remember that Jesus overcame the world. I want to have peace when I think about this. Please help me remember. Help me to keep going forward even when I am suffering.

REFLECT

Think about what it's like to have peace. It's being able to trust God and rest even when things are hard. Write down your thoughts about how you can keep looking to Jesus and trusting that he has overcome the world.

DAY 24
Purpose in the Pain

The Bible shows us that God knows everything and is always wise. But *people* don't know everything. They can't see the future. They can't read other people's minds. They don't always know how to make good decisions. So God and people are very different in this way. If we knew everything God knows, it would be too much for us to handle!

God says,

My thoughts are not your thoughts,
>   neither are your ways my ways, declares the Lord.
For as the heavens are higher than the earth,
>   so are my ways higher than your ways
>   and my thoughts than your thoughts. (Isa. 55:8–9)

God reminds us that we don't understand everything. We may think it would be best if suffering would stop right now. But God sees all the way to the end of our lives. He even sees past when our lives will end. Just as he allowed people in the Bible to suffer, he sometimes lets our suffering continue. But he always has something good planned for us when we keep following him. He knows all things, so he knows what is truly best for us. He uses painful things to help us grow and be closer to him.

One of my favorite passages is Isaiah 61:1–3:

> The Spirit of the Lord God is upon me,
> > because the Lord has anointed me
> to bring good news to the poor;
> > he has sent me to bind up the brokenhearted,
> to proclaim liberty to the captives,
> > and the opening of the prison to those who are bound;
> to proclaim the year of the Lord's favor,
> > and the day of vengeance of our God;
> > to comfort all who mourn;
> to grant to those who mourn in Zion—
> > to give them a beautiful headdress instead of ashes,
> the oil of gladness instead of mourning,
> > the garment of praise instead of a faint spirit;
> that they may be called oaks of righteousness,
> > the planting of the Lord, that he may be glorified.

Jesus our overcomer gives us peace, but he also gives us something else when we keep following him in the midst of our suffering. He gives us his goodness and beauty. He makes us strong like oak trees. We can believe that the God who knows all things always knows best, and he has a purpose in our pain.

So, what if God doesn't answer my prayer for suffering to stop? *You can trust God even when his plans don't make sense to you, knowing that he sent Jesus to save you and give you peace and purpose.*

> **Purpose**
> The reason something is done or created.

PRAYER

Dear Father, I'm glad you know everything. It's hard that I don't understand your plans, but I trust you. Thank you that you give purpose to my pain. Thank you for making me strong and giving me goodness and beauty.

REFLECT

Have you ever noticed that you get stronger when you go through something hard? Think about ways you have grown because of suffering. Write down some ways God has given purpose to your pain.

Question 9

What Gives Someone Hope When Bad Things Keep Happening?

DAY 25

The Greatest Treasure

Do you have anything that you really treasure? I remember begging my parents for a certain doll when I was a little girl. Once I got it, I treasured it. I was careful with it. I didn't let other people play with it. I kept it by my side when I slept. Even after I outgrew it, it was still important to me.

Listen to the words of 2 Corinthians 4:7: "We have this treasure in jars of clay, to show that the surpassing power belongs to God and not to us." Would you keep a valuable treasure in a clay pot? I wouldn't. I would put it somewhere special so nothing bad could happen to it. But God does something different.

People are kind of like clay pots. They don't last forever. They can break or fall apart. But God puts his greatest gift—salvation—into our hearts. This treasure lives in us even though we are breakable. God is showing us that he is more powerful than the things that can harm us.

Here is the next part of this passage: "We are afflicted in every way, but not crushed; perplexed, but not driven to despair; persecuted, but not forsaken; struck down, but not destroyed" (2 Cor. 4:8–9). These verses give examples of bad things that can happen. We can get confused. We can be treated badly by other people. We can be pushed down. But we are never crushed or destroyed. Why? Because the treasure lives in our hearts. And the treasure

> **Treasure**
> Something very valuable to the person who owns or seeks it.

of the gospel—the good news about Jesus—is more powerful than our suffering.

When you give your life to Jesus, you will still have hard times. But no matter what happens, Jesus is alive in you. He has given you eternal life. When this life ends, you will have a life forever with him in heaven. He has also given you hope and comfort in this life. His Holy Spirit teaches you, helps you, and provides for you. The treasure of our salvation in Jesus never gets destroyed.

So what gives someone hope when bad things keep happening? *Suffering is difficult, but it cannot destroy us.*

PRAYER

Dear God, thank you for putting the treasure of salvation into my heart. Please help me to remember this when bad things happen. I want to have hope. Help me believe you and the gospel that cannot be destroyed.

REFLECT

Spend some time thinking about how valuable salvation is. Maybe you can draw or paint a picture of a treasure and write "Salvation" above it. This can help you remember that suffering ultimately cannot destroy you if you are a Christian.

DAY 26

God's Powerful Love

Think about the person you love most. Have you ever had to be separated from that person? Maybe you went to camp and didn't see your parents for several days. Maybe your best friend moved away. It's hard to be separated from people we love. It can feel lonely and very sad.

The treasure of salvation lives inside every Christian. This gives us hope when hard times come. But here's another thing that gives us hope: God's love for us can never be broken or taken away. No matter what bad things happen, God always loves us. He always stays close to us. The Bible tells us about the depth of his love:

> Who shall separate us from the love of Christ? Shall tribulation, or distress, or persecution, or famine, or nakedness, or danger, or sword? . . . No, in all these things we are more than conquerors through him who loved us. For I am sure that neither death nor life, nor angels nor rulers, nor things present nor things to come, nor powers, nor height nor depth, nor anything else in all creation, will be able to separate us from the love of God in Christ Jesus our Lord. (Rom. 8:35, 37–39)

This is a long list! The writer is reminding us that nothing can take away God's love. Absolutely nothing. This is the greatest comfort of all when we are suffering. We will never be alone. God knows we need him, and he never leaves. He is with us no matter what bad things happen. His love is stronger than our suffering.

> **Conqueror**
>
> Someone who overcomes an enemy or wins a war.

This passage says Christians are "more than conquerors." A conqueror is someone who overcomes an enemy or wins a war. We may feel the pain of battle, but the Bible tells us we have won the war against sin and suffering. But it's not because we are awesome. It's because God is awesome, and he has done it for us. He destroyed the power of sin when Jesus died and rose again. And why did he do it? Because he loves us.

So what gives someone hope when bad things keep happening? *Suffering is difficult, but it cannot destroy us or separate us from God's love.*

PRAYER

Dear God, thank you that your love is stronger than my suffering. Please stay close to me and remind me that you love me. Help me to believe you and trust you.

REFLECT

Have you ever thought of yourself as a conqueror? Think about how God's love and salvation make you a conqueror over sin. You can write down some ways that you have felt God's powerful love even in hard times.

DAY 27

Unseen Hope

Have you ever noticed that everything eventually wears out? The toy or bike you got three years ago might be broken now. Your clothes get ripped and dirty. The things in your house stop working after a while. Nothing on this earth lasts forever.

Our bodies don't last forever either. Remember how people are like clay pots? Bones and muscles can break and weaken. Eventually our bodies stop working completely. You may not notice this now. But as you get older, you will start to see your body wearing out.

This is a form of suffering. As things wear down and break, we feel pain. It's hard to have hope when this happens over and over. But God promises that one thing never wears out: "We do not lose heart. Though our outer self is wasting away, *our inner self is being renewed day by day*" (2 Cor. 4:16). Our inner self is where Jesus's Spirit lives. Over time, it keeps growing to be more like Jesus.

Listen to the next part of the passage: "For this light momentary affliction is preparing for us an eternal weight of glory beyond all comparison, as we look not to the things that are seen but to the things that are unseen. For the things that are seen are transient, but the things that are unseen are eternal" (2 Cor. 4:17–18). This is saying that our suffering is not very heavy when we compare it to the hope we have in Jesus. We have hope today, and we also

> **Renew**
> To give fresh life or strength.

have hope that one day all the pain will stop. God will wipe away every tear and make all things good when the new heaven and new earth come (Rev. 21:4).

This doesn't mean our suffering doesn't matter. It means something bigger and better is also happening: Jesus's love lives inside us and *renews* us. It keeps giving us strength and making us wiser.

If you look at a picture of the earth, you can see how big it is. But if you look at a picture of the entire galaxy, you hardly see the earth. It's just a tiny dot. God's word tells us to look at the gift of Jesus's amazing and powerful love. When we do, it's like looking at the whole galaxy. And that reminds us that even though our pain is big, it can never be as big as Jesus's love.

So what gives someone hope when bad things keep happening? *Suffering is difficult, but it cannot destroy us or separate us from God's love, which renews our hearts and leads us to our heavenly home.*

PRAYER

Dear Lord, thank you that your love and salvation are so much bigger than my suffering. Help me to keep looking at you when I am in pain. Help me to trust you and look forward to the day when all suffering will end.

REFLECT

Write down some of the hard things you experience. Then write down some things you've learned in this book about God's gifts to you. You can even draw pictures of God's gifts. You can remember the hard things, but you also need to remember how big God's love is.

Question 10

How Can I Help Someone Else Who Is Suffering?

DAY 28

The Light of God's Love

If you had to draw a picture of love, what would you draw? Maybe you'd draw a big heart or a picture of two people hugging. Love can be hard to define. It's a feeling but also a commitment. When you love others, you keep spending time with them. You stay close to them because they are important to you.

The Bible draws us its own picture of love. First John 4:8 says, "God is love." This is a big deal. It doesn't just say God has love—it says he *is* love. God is the definition of what love is. We can see this when we read stories about Jesus. He healed people. He helped them understand God. And most of all, he gave himself by dying on the cross for our sin.

Let's read 1 John 4:11–12: "Beloved, if God so loved us, we also ought to love one another. No one has ever seen God; if we love one another, God abides in us and his love is perfected in us." God loved us so much that he gave his Son to us (see John 3:16). He did the hardest thing possible so we could have a relationship with him. And he wants us to reflect his love to other people.

Here's an example that might help you understand this. You have learned in school that the sun is the source of light and heat for the earth. Without it, we wouldn't be able to live. But what about the moon? It doesn't make its own heat or light. When we

> **Love**
> A deep feeling of affection, care, and devotion to someone.

see the moon in the sky, we are seeing the light of the sun bouncing off the moon.

In this example, God is like the sun. He is the source of love. We are like the moon. We take in God's love, and it makes us alive. We *abide* in his love, which means we keep receiving it. And then we reflect it onto other people. So if you want to love someone who is suffering, you can receive God's love and then show it to that person. In the next two days, we'll talk about how you can show love to other people when they suffer.

So how can I help someone else who is suffering? *You can reflect God's love to others.*

PRAYER

Dear Father, thank you for loving me. Please help me reflect your love to other people when they are suffering. Help me to point people to you as the source of love.

REFLECT

Think about the illustration of the sun and moon. Now think about how God's love shines on you. How do you know he loves you? You can write down your thoughts or share them with someone you trust.

DAY 29
God Shows Us How

When others suffer, we should reflect God's love to them. But how can we do that? What should we say? To help us answer this question, let's remember what God does for us when we suffer. In Question 7 we learned that God is a comforter. Because God comforts us, we can comfort each other.

God's word says, "Blessed be the God and Father of our Lord Jesus Christ, the Father of mercies and God of all comfort, who comforts us in all our affliction, so that we may be able to comfort those who are in any affliction, with the comfort with which we ourselves are comforted by God" (2 Cor. 1:3–4). These verses remind us that God is our comforter. He teaches us how to comfort other people by the way he comforts us.

Think back to when you were learning to write. You didn't learn just by looking at the letters. Someone had to show you how to actually do it. Your teacher may have even held the pencil with you and guided your hand through the motions. You learned how to write because she *modeled* it—she taught you by showing you.

God models how we can comfort others. He teaches us by comforting us. The way he comforts us is the way we can comfort other people. The Bible shows us that God *listens*, and he *comes close*. We can do both of these things for other people.

You might not know what to say when someone is suffering, but there is good news! You don't have to say something to make a friend feel better. You will help him feel better by listening and com-

> **Comfort**
> The easing of someone's pain.

ing close, like God does for you. All you have to say is something like, "I'm sorry you're in pain. I want to be here for you." And then you can listen. If he doesn't want to talk, that's ok. There will probably be time for talking later. For now, you can just be close. This will show him that you care, and it will reflect God's love to him.

There are also many other ways you can show love to people when they are suffering. You can do something kind for them. You can invite them to spend time with you. Comfort comes in all shapes and sizes.

So how can I help someone else who is suffering? *You can reflect God's love and comfort to others.*

PRAYER

Dear Lord, thank you for comforting me and showing me how to comfort others. Please help me to be loving and kind when others are in pain. Show me how I can love them.

REFLECT

Think about your friends and family members. Are any suffering right now? How have you listened and come close to them? Maybe you can think of ways to comfort them and pray for them.

DAY 30
Keep Going to the End

Have you ever been on a long hike? Hiking takes perseverance. *Perseverance* means you keep going for a long time. You don't give up. Even when you get tired, you walk till the hike ends. This life is like a long hike. It takes perseverance. And when suffering happens, it gets really hard to keep going. But we are not alone. God is with us. He gives us strength for the journey.

Caring for others who are suffering is like hiking with them. It's hard work, but we can reflect God's love by joining them on their journey. Listen to Ephesians 4:1–2: "I therefore, a prisoner for the Lord, urge you to walk in a manner worthy of the calling to which you have been called, with all humility and gentleness, with patience, bearing with one another in love." What is our calling? As Christians, we are called to love God and love other people. We do this with gentleness and patience.

What does it mean to *bear with one another*? Picture the hike again. Bearing with someone is like hiking with a friend when she is walking very slowly. Maybe she has a twisted ankle, or maybe her backpack is too heavy. She can't go very fast, so you walk beside her. You choose to stay close so that she won't be alone. You are patient and gentle. This is what God does for us, isn't it? He stays close to us when we are hiking slowly through life.

> **Perseverance**
> Continuing to do something even when it's difficult or slow.

Another way you can bear with others is to pray for them. Praying for people who are suffering shows God's love to them. And God hears our prayers! He wants us to pray for each other (see James 5:16). And he wants us to keep praying, even when suffering keeps happening. Prayer also takes perseverance. That means you keep praying even when it's hard.

As you have learned throughout this book, suffering is difficult. But God loves us. He is with us. And he shows us how to keep going and how to help others keep going. We will make it to the end of this journey, because he loves us and promises to be with us till the end.

So how can I help someone else who is suffering? *You can reflect God's love and comfort to others with patience and gentleness.*

PRAYER

Dear God, you have shown me how to keep going through suffering. You have shown me how to help someone else who is suffering. Thank you for your love. Thank you that you will be with me to the end of this journey.

REFLECT

Think back through what you have learned in this book. What stood out to you the most? What can you share with someone else? Think about writing down some things that will help you remember God's love when you are suffering.

Key Words About Pain and Suffering

burden: A heavy load that someone carries.

comfort: The easing of someone's pain.

complaint: A statement that a situation is difficult or painful.

conqueror: Someone who overcomes an enemy or wins a war.

consequence: The result of a sinful or harmful action.

corruption: The process of decay because of sin, becoming worse and worse over time.

discipline: The practice of training people to obey and make wise choices.

fallen: The state of the world after Adam and Eve sinned; a state of hardship, sin, and suffering.

glorify: To celebrate and describe someone as wonderful and worthy.

helper: Someone who supports someone else.

hope: A feeling of strong confidence in a person or circumstance.

Immanuel: One of the names given to Jesus. It means "God with us."

inheritance: A gift you receive after a loved one's death.

just: Behaving according to what is right and fair.

keeper: A person who manages or looks after something or someone.

love: A deep feeling of affection, care, and devotion to someone.

oppress: To cause someone else to feel pain or distress.

overcome: To succeed in defeating an enemy or problem.

perseverance: Continuing to do something even when it's difficult or slow.

power: The ability to be strong and do something to cause change.

protection: Keeping someone safe from harm or danger.

punishment: The penalty for doing something wrong.

purpose: The reason something is done or created.

renew: To give fresh life or strength.

sin: Doing wrong in disobedience to God.

steadfastness: The quality of being firm, strong, and unchanging.

suffering: The state of experiencing pain or distress.

treasure: Something very valuable to the person who owns or seeks it.

waiting: The action of staying where you are until something else happens.

wisdom: The quality of having experience, knowledge, and good judgment.

10 Questions About Pain and Suffering (with Answers)

1. What is suffering?

Suffering is the experience of pain that everyone feels, because sin caused suffering to enter the world. But suffering doesn't last forever for Christians because God sent his Son into the world to suffer with us and rescue us.

2. Why do we suffer?

Sometimes we suffer as a consequence of our sin, sometimes we suffer when other people sin, and sometimes we suffer because we live in a fallen world.

3. If God is good, why does he let bad things happen?

Suffering reminds us of our deep problem of sin and that the world is under the devil's limited power, but God creates good things through bad things.

4. Do Christians suffer less than non-Christians?

Christians do not suffer less than non-Christians because all humans experience both good and evil, but Christians have a Helper and a strong hope in our suffering.

5. When Christians suffer, is it punishment?

No. For anyone who believes in him, Jesus has taken the punishment that sinners deserve; God wants to grow us, not punish us, and his glory is shown as he helps and heals us.

6. How does God help me when I'm suffering?

God comes near, and he gives strength, protection, and wisdom.

7. How should Christians respond to suffering?

Through prayer, we seek comfort from God and help from other people, always holding on to the hope of heaven.

8. What if God doesn't answer my prayer for suffering to stop?

You can trust God even when his plans don't make sense to you, knowing that he sent Jesus to save you and give you peace and purpose.

9. What gives someone hope when bad things keep happening?

Suffering is difficult, but it cannot destroy us or separate us from God's love, which renews our hearts and leads us to our heavenly home.

10. How can I help someone else who is suffering?

You can reflect God's love and comfort to others with patience and gentleness.

10 QUESTIONS SERIES

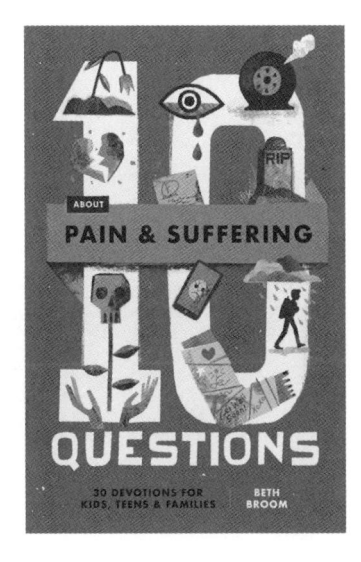

For more information, visit **crossway.org**.